Budgeting and Money Management -The Basics

A Lifelong Plan for Managing Your Money

by

Neil Bryan

Book 1: Money Action Plan Series

Dedication

To Maureen

Table of Contents

Budgeting and Money Management - The Basics

My Story

In 1985, I was thirty-eight years old, unemployed and had not saved a penny toward retirement. I was living with my wife and two sons in a rented house and had considerable credit card debt. We had two old used cars and not much else.

Retirement looked like it was going to be a long way off for me.

About the time things were at the lowest point, we decided to put together a plan for getting out of debt, buying a house, buying a new car and getting on the road to retirement. Together, my wife and I designed the plan that is the subject of this book.

Today, 2014, I am retired with a decent pension, a sufficient IRA balance and adequate other investments.

Now, before you make the assumption that everything was easy after we designed the plan, consider where I was at age thirty-eight; deep in debt, no job, no pension, no investments, no house of my own. The recommendation at that time was that a married couple needed $1,000,000 in order to retire comfortably. I thought that was an impossible amount to accumulate, with the debt, college expenses, daily living expenses, possible mortgage for a house, car payments, etc.

It was enough to make us want to give up. But we didn't. We stuck to the plan until we finally saw some results. The early results encouraged us to continue with the plan.

In the early years it required some scrimping and saving money on everything we bought but it has been worth it. We would go grocery shopping with a stack of coupons and usually save up to fifty percent on our total grocery bill. I know there are people who save even more than that. The hardest part was controlling the budget so that eventually we had an excess each month that we could put away toward other things.

The key to this plan is being consistent in using the money management techniques that are presented in this book, being diligent in using the plan and not giving up.

Consistency is what wins the money game.

WHY I WROTE THIS BOOK

You may wonder why I wrote this book. After all, we succeeded in getting to retirement. Why bother to tell other people what we learned along the way and share valuable information that we have accumulated. Here's the simple truth; we believe anyone can use this plan for managing their finances, making financial decisions and retiring comfortably. This is a plan for life and the earlier you start it the better off you will be later on in life. I started when I was thirty-eight and I'm comfortably retired now at the age of sixty-eight. Just imagine if you started in your twenties how much better off you would be when you're ready for retirement.

Budgeting and Money Management - The Basics

The goal of this book is to give any person, whether you're a high school dropout or have a PhD, the exact steps necessary to get their financial life under control. By the way, I know many highly educated people who are very poor with money. I also know many less educated people who understand what they need to do to manage their money. Education should not be a problem. The desire to get control of your money is the only requirement.

So many other books and websites we've looked at simply bombard the reader with financial information but give no clue as to how to apply any of the information they supply. This simply leads to information overload and leaves the reader out in the cold as to what to do first, second, third, etc.

With that in mind, we will give you the exact steps you must take to create your own personal Money Action Plan (MAP), manage it, measure its effectiveness and, most importantly, understand what you are doing and why.

The MAP will help you take control of your money for life. It's a plan I've been using for almost 30 years and you too can use it for your entire life. I know money doesn't buy happiness but not having enough money can cause some serious stress in your life.

WHAT THIS BOOK IS

In addition to being a companion book to the Money Action Plan software, this book is a detailed step by step guide starting with an evaluation of your income and expenses, through creating and managing your budget and tracking your Net-Worth. Investing, retirement planning and estate planning are covered in additional books. You need to get your money under control first. This book is written primarily for the beginner but can be used by anyone. Along the way, I will educate you on financial terms, concepts and language so you will better understand what you are doing and you are better prepared to make the important financial decisions you will need to make throughout your life.

This is a lifelong plan for your money, a Money Action Plan

Each step in this process builds on previous steps. Pertinent information will be supplied as needed to explain financial concepts and help you understand exactly why something needs to be done.

WHAT THIS BOOK IS NOT

This is not a get rich quick scheme. I won't be telling you how you can make thousands of dollars a day or a week clipping coupons or selling online, doing piece work in your garage or writing eBooks or any of the other unbelievably fantastic offers I've seen. While some of these are certainly legitimate ways to make some income or reduce expenses, they may or may not be right for you.

REMEMBER, if it's too good to be true, it's probably not true.

DISCLAIMER:
I am not a Certified Financial Planner or a CPA or an Attorney.

What I do have are a Bachelor's Degree in Business Administration and an MBA along with over forty years of experience in the financial and computer systems fields.

In this book and the ones that follow in the Money Action Plan Series, I am simply presenting what has worked for me over the last thirty years. This is really a formalization of the methods I have been using including the software. I have been using spreadsheets for my budgeting and the Money Action Plan software is the first time the process has been formalized into a software system to be offered to the public.

As far as any websites mentioned in the book, they are for illustration purposes only. I am not a principal in any company mentioned. The only exception to this is www.moneyactionplan.com in which I am a principal owner. Investment companies mentioned are ones that I use or have used in the past but the reader is free to use any company they wish.

While I strongly believe this system will help anyone get their money under control, I cannot guarantee that it will. Some will find the process too cumbersome or will not want to put in the time to learn and do what is suggested. Individual results will certainly vary based on the commitment of the user.

Software

At this time, the software is unsupported but thoroughly tested so that it performs as described in the book. It is free and can always be downloaded again if the user gets into a problem they can't resolve.

If you uncover any issues or have any suggestions, please use the Comment / Inquiry Form on the website at www.moneyactionplan.com explaining the issue or suggestion and we will see what we can do about it. We're always looking to get better.

HOW TO USE THIS BOOK AND SOFTWARE

You may be wondering how exactly this system can be described as the basics. Because it is! Don't let the number of pages fool or discourage you into thinking that you can never do this.

A lot of the information in this book is for your use as you get more familiar with the concepts of Budgeting and Money Management.

You should concentrate on the Budgeting aspect of the system first because this is really where you will gain control of your money. The Money Management part of the system consists of what you do on a consistent basis to maintain control and shape your future by eventually investing, creating a formal retirement plan and properly planning for your estate.

Here is the exact order in which you should read this book and use the software.

Budgeting and Money Management - The Basics

1. Read and understand "Overview: What You Will Learn"

2. Read and understand "Explanation of the Software". As part of this, download the software so you can start familiarizing yourself with it. You can download the free software at www.moneyactionplan.com.

3. Spend some time playing with the software so you know what it does and where to find what you need.

4. Read "Create Your Budget Snapshot" and follow the instructions to do this.

5. Read "Data Gathering: The Heart of Budget and Money Management" and apply what you learn about recording your actual income and expenses for the month.

6. Read "What to do with the Budget Excess or Shortage" so you will know that at the end of the month you have some decisions to make

to develop the control necessary for your Money Action Plan to succeed.

7. Read "Preparing for Next Month" to see how easy it will be to take the data you have collected for the current month and use it to create your budget for the next month.

8. Read "Managing the Process" for the steps that you need to take on a daily, weekly, monthly and yearly basis.

Only after your first month is complete (meaning you created a budget and entered all the actual income and expense for the month, reviewed the Budget Summary and took the necessary action on either the Budget Excess Planning form or the Budget Shortage Planning form):

9. Read "Revising Your Starting Budget Amounts"

10. Read "Review and Maximize your Income". There is a lot of information and tips about

how to review your income and what to look for in book 2 of the Money Action Plan Series, <u>Keep More of What You Earn</u>. This book is designed as a resource for you to go to when you have the time to work on some of the concepts and ideas presented.

11. Read "Review and Minimize your Expenses". The same applies to this as the one above regarding reviewing you income.

Only after you feel you have your Budget under control (meaning you know how to budget, how to record your actual expenses and deal with the excess or shortage each month and you have performed the reviews of income and expenses mentioned above)

12. Read "List Your Assets" and follow the instructions to complete this.

13. Read "List Your Liabilities" and follow the instructions to complete this.

14. Print and Review your Net-Worth Statement as part of the monthly reports that you print for your records.

15. Start Over

OVERVIEW: WHAT YOU WILL LEARN

Here is a summary of all that you will learn from this book while on your journey to create your Money Action Plan.

SOFTWARE

You will learn how to use the downloadable software provided as part of this book that can be used to do all of what's described below. This will simplify the entire process and help you stay on track with your Money Action Plan.

FIRST: BUDGET SNAPSHOT, STARTING BUDGET, FINAL BUDGET, DATA GATHERING

You will complete a **Budget Snapshot** by listing all your income and expenses. This sounds simple and is. Your actual listed income and expense becomes your **Starting Budget** and for the first month, your **Final Budget**. For the first month, this is all you do. For the second month and beyond, your starting budget is based on the previous month's actual income and expense that you record on the *Data Gathering Form*.

SECOND: INCOME AND EXPENSE REVIEW
You will review all of your income items and all of your expense items with the goal of maximizing your income and minimizing your expense. Any changes you make can be put into practice as you review and make decisions about each income and expense item. This step is optional but highly recommended. I think you'll be surprised by what you can accomplish with this.

THIRD: BUDGET SUMMARY, EXCESS PLANNING, SHORTAGE PLANNING
You will learn how to deal with a budget shortage or budget excess, i.e. what to do if you are short of money for your budget or have extra money at the end of the month. This process is helped along by the completion of the *Budget Excess Planning form* or *Budget Shortage Planning form*, both of which are provided in the software. The software includes

a **Budget Summary** that presents your budget in summary format, compares it with your actual income and expenses and offers suggestions as to what to do next to keep you Money Action Plan on track.

FOURTH: MANAGING THE PROCESS
You will learn how to manage this process on a daily, weekly, monthly and annual basis to keep your money growing and establish a real lifetime Money Action Plan.

FIFTH: ASSETS
You will identify and learn what the different categories of assets are and List Your Assets in preparation for creating your Net-Worth Statement.

SIXTH: LIABILITIES
You will identify and learn what the different categories of liabilities are and List Your Liabilities in preparation for creating you Net-Worth Statement.

SEVENTH: NET-WORTH

You will create a *Net-Worth Statement*; learn what it is and how it will be used to measure your progress. This will include listing all your assets and liabilities. Don't worry; everything will be explained as we go through the plan.

OBJECTIVES

So, let's get started getting your finances on track and creating your own personal Money Action Plan – the MAP for your financial life.

These are the objectives of the first part of the Money Action Plan system. I call this the core of the plan. It is what you need to keep in mind every day as you move forward with your plan. All this will be explained in detail as we proceed with the plan.

These are the Objectives to achieve:

Create Your Budget Snapshot

Create an estimate of your income for the month

Budgeting and Money Management - The Basics

Create an estimate of what expenses you have for the month

Know if you will be short of money or have extra money for the month before the month starts

Have a budget plan for dealing with the shortage or what you will do with the extra money

At month end, Create a Net-Worth Statement, know what it is and what it shows.

Manage your budget to maximize your income and minimize your expenses

Here is a description of each of the steps you will take so you will have a good understanding of the entire Money Action Plan process and where you're headed.

Step 1 – Create Your Budget Snapshot
The first step is to create a Budget Snapshot by simply listing all of your income and all of your

expenses for the last complete month. In other words, if you are doing this on December 17, list all your income and expenses for the month of November.

This step should not be very difficult if you use your pay stubs and check book. It may be somewhat more difficult if you don't have a checking account and pay all your bills in cash or by money order.

Step 2 - Create Your Budget

The second step is to analyze and make appropriate modifications to your Income and Expense amounts to produce a budget for the up-coming month.

Step 3 - Manage Your Monthly Budget

The third step is to make sure you take the proper steps to manage your budget monthly and use the information to create your next month's budget.

Step 4 – Create Your Net-Worth Statement

Money Action Plan software:

Before we go any further, if you haven't done so yet, you can download the software for the Money Action Plan system at www.moneyactionplan.com. It is free. At this time it only comes in a Microsoft Excel version.

If you don't have a computer or don't want to use a computer version, then you can do this on a paper spreadsheet. However, it will be a lot more time consuming for you to keep up and manage it. That's why we recommend you download the free software. We had to do it on paper spreadsheets at first because we didn't have and couldn't afford a computer.

Another possibility is to have someone you know download the software and put it on some type of media (a cd, thumb drive, jump drive, flash drive etc) so you can use it at a public computer, such as in a library. Of course the library will need to have

Budgeting and Money Management - The Basics

Microsoft Excel for you to use the Money Action Plan software.

The next chapter is a brief tour of the Money Action Plan software. The software will help you with each of the steps in the plan.

EXPLANATION OF THE SOFTWARE

The software that this Money Action Plan system uses was designed in Microsoft Excel. It can be downloaded from the Money Action Plan website.

To download the software, go to www.moneyactionplan.com

You must register on the Forum Page before you will be allowed to download the software.

Once you have registered, go to the download page, sign in and click the link for the Money Action Plan Software.

After it is downloaded, you may want to use the Save As button to save it to a different location, rather than have it in your download folder.

You should then be all set to use the Money Action Plan software.

Budgeting and Money Management - The Basics

A Brief Tour of the Money Action Plan
Software

So now let's look at all the features of the Money
Action Plan software.

Here is the Main Menu:

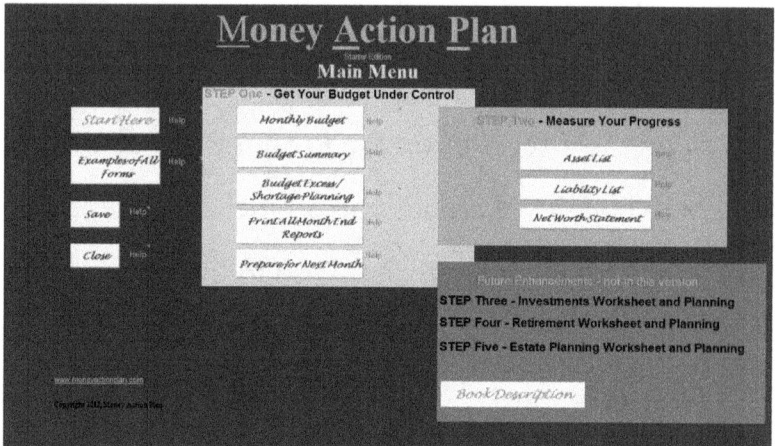

These are the features and purposes of each of the
buttons on the menu.

Forms Available in the FREE Money Action
Plan Software – Starter Edition

- Monthly Budget Worksheet
- Budget Snapshot

Budgeting and Money Management - The Basics

- Data Gathering Form
- Asset List
- Liability List
- Net-Worth Statement
- Budget Summary
- Budget Excess Planning Form
- Budget Shortage Planning Form

BUTTON DESCRIPTIONS:

Start Here - This will give you some basic information about the MAP system and access to the Quick Start Instructions for STEP One and STEP Two.

Example of All forms - Here you can print examples of all the forms used in the MAP system.

Save - This will save the current Money Action Plan system worksheets.

Close - This will close the Money Action Plan System

Save As – This is the same as save but it allows you to save to a different location (such as a portable jump drive).

STEP ONE – GET YOUR BUDGET UNDER CONTROL

Monthly Budget Worksheet - NOTE: This is where you spend the majority of your time in the Money Action Plan software.
Use the Monthly Budget Worksheet to finalize your monthly budget, gather your actual income and expenses for the month and get your budget under control.

Budget Summary - Use the Budget Summary at the end of the month to help determine what to do to manage you budget.
This also provides access to the Budget Excess Planning form and the Budget Shortage Planning Form.

Budget Excess/Shortage Planning Form - Based on whether there is an excess or shortage of income as shown on the Budget Summary, use the proper form to plan for resolving the issue.

Prepare All Reports - Prints the following reports for your records at the end of each month:

> Monthly Budget Worksheet
>
> Data Gathering Form
>
> Budget Summary
>
> Budget Excess Planning Form
>
> Budget Shortage Planning Form
>
> Asset / Liability / Net-Worth Form

Prepare for Next Month - The Prepare for Next Month button performs several actions to set you up for the next budget month as follows:

It Copies the actual income and expense amounts to the Budget Snapshot column of the Monthly Budget Worksheet. This lets you start your budget based on what actually happened in the previous month.

It Clears the Data Gathering Form

It Clears the Budget Adjustment Section of the Monthly Budget Worksheet

It Increments the Month and the Year if necessary.

It sets all codes to "m" meaning monthly because these are all last months amounts.

STEP TWO – MEASURE YOUR PROGRESS

Asset List - Use the Asset List to list all of your assets in the proper categories. This is part of your Net-Worth Statement

Liability List - Use the Liability List to list all the balances on all the accounts you owe. This is the second part of your Net-Worth Statement.

Net-Worth Statement - The Net-Worth Statement is automatically created from what you listed on your Asset and Liability Lists. This can be used as a measurement of your progress in your Money Action Plan.

That's it as far as what is available in the Money Action Plan software. To familiarize yourself with the software, spend some time exploring so you will know how to use the software before you begin. Certain functions of the software will be explained in the chapters that follow.

The Details

Now, let's look at the details of how to do each step.

CREATE YOUR BUDGET SNAPSHOT

PREPARATION:
Gather together information about all your income sources and all your expenses for the month. For income, this could include pay stubs from all jobs that you have, information about other income received (such as regular gifts from parents or others, sales of personal items on ebay or other websites, alimony or child support, etc. In short any money that you receive during any given month should be listed. What is listed should be regular income that you receive and you can rely on to pay your bills each month. Anything else is a windfall.

LIST YOUR INCOME
So what exactly is considered income? Here are some examples of income that should be included in your Budget Snapshot.

- Income from work

- Bonuses from work
- Gifts of money
- Dividends and Interest from Non-Retirement Investments, meaning you receive the money and can use it to pay bills.
- Proceeds from sale of anything
- Alimony received
- Child support received
- Windfalls – any unexpected money received during the month should be considered a windfall and listed in the actual income for the month on the Data Gathering Form. By doing this, you will have that money for the month end process of dealing with an overage or shortage for the month.

Let me emphasize the following: ***This list is intended to cover ALL income you receive or may receive during the month***. NO Exceptions!! Just because you don't find what you have received on this list doesn't mean that it is not income to be considered for your monthly budget. Don't try to cheat the system.

On the Money Action Plan Main Menu (shown below), select Monthly Budget Worksheet and record all this information in the Budget Snapshot section.

In the Budget Snapshot section, list your income by entering a description and amount for each item of income as shown in this example.

Monthly Budget Worksheet

November	2014	Budget Snapshot

Budgeted Income:

Description		Take Home	Code
Take Home Amount;			Help
Paycheck 1	Husband check 1	310	o
Paycheck 2	Husband	350	o
Paycheck 3	Husband	310	o
Paycheck 4	Husband	350	o
Paycheck 5	Wife	240	t
Paycheck 6	Wife	170	t
Paycheck 7	Husband - 2nd Job	80	t
Paycheck 8	Husband - 2nd Job	70	t
Paycheck 9	Wife - babysitting	80	m
Paycheck 10	Wife - 2nd job	130	m
Paycheck 11			m
Paycheck 12			m

Other Income during Month:			Help
Alimony			m
Child Support		110	w
Gifts			m
Sale of personal items			m
			m
			m

Pay particular attention to the code to the right of the amount. You must enter the proper code (explained below) so the software can calculate your Starting Budget Amount.

Codes Explanation:

Enter one of these codes for each line to describe how often you receive this income:

d = this income amount is received daily

w = this income amount is received weekly (same amount each week),

o (the letter o) = this income amount is received once each month (use if take home pay is different each week)

m = this income amount is received monthly

t = this income amount is received twice a month if the same amount each time, otherwise use Code o

n = this income amount is received at no set frequency

Your income can be listed using your weekly, bi-weekly or monthly pay stubs. Be sure you list the Net Amount, the amount you actually took home and is available to you for spending. For now, we will ignore your gross amount, which is the amount before any deductions for taxes, insurance, 401k, etc.

Be sure you also list any other income that you receive during the month. This should only be income that you regularly receive not one-time gifts or refunds, etc.

As you enter each line of income, the Starting Budget Amount will be calculated by the software based on the code that you enter.

After you are finished with this first step, your spreadsheet should look something like this Completed Income Example:

Budgeting and Money Management - The Basics

Monthly Budget Worksheet

November 2014

	Budget Snapshot	

Budgeted Income:

Description		Take Home	Code	Starting Budget Amounts
Take Home Amount;			*Help*	
Paycheck 1	*Husband check 1*	310	o	335
Paycheck 2	*Husband*	350	o	378
Paycheck 3	*Husband*	310	o	335
Paycheck 4	*Husband*	350	o	378
Paycheck 5	*Wife*	240	t	521
Paycheck 6	*Wife*	170	t	369
Paycheck 7	*Husband - 2nd Job*	80	t	174
Paycheck 8	*Husband - 2nd Job*	70	t	152
Paycheck 9	*Wife - babysitting*	80	m	80
Paycheck 10	*Wife - 2nd job*	130	m	130
Paycheck 11			m	0
Paycheck 12			m	0
Other Income during Month:			*Help*	
Alimony			m	0
Child Support		110	w	476
Gifts			m	0
Sale of personal items			m	0
			m	0
			m	0
Total Spendable Income for Month				3328

NOTE:

Starting Budget Calculation: The Starting Budget is calculated on an annual basis using the code you entered for the income line item. For example, because there are 52 weeks in 12 months, there are

39

actually 4.333 weeks per month. The first item shows income of $310 once during the month. This amount multiplied by 4.333 is $335, the actual amount you receive during a one month period. Another example, the wife's 2nd job income ($80) is coded as t, meaning this income is received twice a month. This works out to $40 a week, multiplied by 4.33 equals approximately $174 a month.

Don't let these calculations get you off track. You really don't have to concern yourself with this since the software does it for you.

LIST YOUR EXPENSES

So what exactly is an expense? It seems fairly obvious but let's just make sure we're all talking about the same thing. Here are some examples of expenses.

This should include all expenses that you pay on a regular monthly basis such as mortgage payments, rent, groceries, child care, other loan payments, credit card payments, etc. If a bill is paid only a couple times a year such as real estate tax, just include it in the budget in the month in which it will be paid.

Checks written for payment of bills

- On-line Banking Payments of bills
- Cash payment of bills
- Cash withdrawals including ATM withdrawals
- Any other charges to checking account such as;

- Insurance payments
- Other Loan payments
- Child support payments
- Alimony payments
- Credit Card Payments
- Mortgage Payments
- Other Loans Payments
- Home Improvement Loans
- Car Loans
- Furniture Loans
- Payday Loans

Again, your expense may not be on this list but that does not mean it is not an expense that should be considered in your monthly budget. There are NO Exceptions to the money you spend each month. *If you spent it or intend to spend it, then it should be part of your monthly budget.*

Notice that the budget expense area is divided into daily, weekly and monthly sections. This is strictly for you convenience in completing the form.

For instance, the example of Child Care listed in the weekly section could be daily or monthly. Also, the Cash Allowances listed as weekly could be daily or monthly.

It all depends on how you do it.

The Code column controls the Starting Budget calculation regardless of the section where the expense is listed.

It is easy to change an expense from daily to weekly simply by changing the code from d to w.

After completion, this should look something like this only with your personal data included;

Expenses Example:

Budgeted Expenses:

Description	Amount	Code	Starting Budget Amounts
Daily: (Average)		Help	
Meals – outside of home	6	d	180
Misc (Newspaper, etc)	1	d	30
Coffee	2	d	60
		d	0
		d	0
		d	0
		d	0
Weekly		Help	
Gas	40	v	173
Food	300	v	1299
Cash Allowance – Husband	50	v	217
Cash Allowance – Wife	50	v	217
Cash Allowance – 3 Children	45	v	195
Child Care	150	v	650
		v	0
		v	0
		v	0
		v	0
		v	0
		v	0
Monthly:		Help	
Mortgage / Rent	600	m	600
Car Payment	320	m	320
Phone – Home Phone and Cells	200	m	200
Heating Oil	300	m	300
Electricity	140	m	140
Internet	60	m	60
House Insurance	450	m	450
Life Insurance	270	m	270
Cable TV	120	m	120
		m	0
		m	0
		m	0

Total Expenses for Month   5481

Plus = Excess / (Minus) = Shortage   (2153)

Note that in this example, the Total Spendable Income for the budget month is $3328 but the Total Budgeted Expenses for the budget month is $5481.

44

As the budget sheet shows, this is a shortage of $2153 for the month. We will talk in more detail about this shortage and what to do about it in the next chapter, Revising Your Starting Budget Amounts.

Once you have completed listing your income and expenses on the Budget Snapshot, you are done with this step.

As you can see, preparing your Budget Snapshot is nothing more than listing your monthly income and monthly expenses. So, why do we do this? It's simple. We need a starting point for getting your finances in order and the Budget Snapshot is that starting point.

Budgeting and Money Management - The Basics

REVISING YOUR STARTING BUDGET AMOUNTS

NOTE: This step is optional for now if you want to just use the amounts you input as your first budget and get through the first month before you do anything else.

If you are using our Money Action Plan spreadsheet system, your Starting Budget Amounts have been calculated based on what you input for income and expenses.

The Starting Budget Amount column shows what you estimate will be your income and expenses for the month.

Next, you can do a complete review of your income and expense and make any changes on the Budget Snapshot in the appropriate column. These review procedures are explained in detail in the following

Budgeting and Money Management - The Basics

chapters: <u>Review and Maximize Your Income</u> and <u>Review and Minimize Your Expenses</u>.

This is a sample of what Budget revisions to income looks like:

Monthly Budget Worksheet	Sample Form					
November 2014	Budget Snapshot		Budget Adjustment			
		Starting Budget Amounts	Adjust Amount To:	Reason for Changing	Final Budget Amounts	
Budgeted Income:						
Description	Take Home	Code				
Paycheck Take Home Amounts;		Help				
Husband check 1	310	o	335	350	Change W4	350
Husband	350	o	378			378
Husband	310	o	335			335
Husband	350	o	378			378
Wife	240	t	521			521
Wife	170	t	369			369
Husband - 2nd Job	80	t	174			174
Husband - 2nd Job	70	t	152			152
Wife - babysitting	80	m	80			80
Wife - 2nd job	130	m	130	0	Company closed	0
		m	0			0
		m	0			0
Other Income during Month:		Help				
Alimony		m	0			0
Child support	110	w	476	380	Received advance l	380
Gifts		m	0			0
Sale of personal items		m	0	800	Sell Snowmobile	800
		m	0			0
		m	0			0
Total Spendable Income for Month			3328			3917

This is a sample of what Budget revisions to expenses looks like:

Monthly Budget Worksheet *Sample Form*

November 2014 | Budget Snapshot | **Budget Adjustment**

NOTE: The Daily, Weekly and Monthly Sections are for illustration purposes only. The real software does not have these. You use the Code to indicate how often the expense occurs.

Budgeted Expenses: Description	Amount	Code	Starting Budget Amounts	Adjust Amount To:	Reason for Changing	Final Budget Amounts
Daily: (Average)		Help				
Meals - outside of home	6	d	180	0	Take lunch	0
Misc (Newspaper, etc)	1	d	30	0	Read at office	0
Coffee	2	d	60	0	Get coffee at office	0
		d	0			0
		d	0			0
		d.	0			0
		d	0			0
Weekly		Help				
Gas	40	w	173	40	Car pool	40
Food	300	w	1299	1000	Coupons	1000
Cash Allowance - Husband	50	w	217	150	Reduce allowance	150
Cash Allowance - Wife	50	w	217	100	Reduce allowance	100
Cash Allowance - 3 Children	45	w	195	60	Reduce allowance	60
Child Care	150	w	650			650
		w	0			0
		w	0			0
		w	0			0
		w	0			0
		w	0			0
		w	0			0
Monthly:		Help				
Mortgage / Rent	600	m	600			600
Car Payment	320	m	320			320
Phone - Home Phone and Cells	200	m	200	120	Change plan	120
Heating Oil	300	m	300	250	Reduce thermostat	250
Electricity	140	m	140	120	Turn off lights, tvs,	120
Internet	60	m	60	45	Change plan	45
House Insurance	450	m	450	0	Not due this month	0
Life Insurance	270	m	270	0	Cancel Insurance	0
Cable TV	120	m	120			120
		m	0			0
		m	0			0
		m	0			0
Total Expenses for Month			5481			3575
Plus = Excess / (Minus) = Shortage			(2153)			342

These adjustments should be based on your knowledge of what you can do to help balance your budget. You shouldn't just put in adjustments that don't make sense or cannot possibly be accomplished within the month.

For your first budget, concentrate on the Daily and Weekly expenses identified on the expense budget. This is where you will probably find the most changes you can make to immediately impact and improve your budget.

The ultimate goal every month is to have the bottom line, "Plus = Excess / (Minus) = Shortage" be a positive number in the Final Budget Column. This means you have extra money that will require a decision on your part as to what to do with the extra. The Budget Summary along with the Budget Excess or Budget Shortage Planning Form will help with any decisions you need to make.

DATA GATHERING: THE HEART OF BUDGET AND MONEY MANAGEMENT

PREPARATION FOR DATA GATHERING

The Money Action Plan software provides a Data Gathering Form. This is used for two purposes:

Gather your actual Income and Expense Data for the month

Use this actual data as a basis for your next months Starting Budget

By doing this consistently month after month, you will be fine tuning your budgeting process and moving toward properly managing your money for the long term.

USING THE DATA GATHERING FORM

You can print the Data Gathering Form for the month you are working on after you have completed your budget and settled on your Final Budget amounts. By printing this out you will be able to write down income and expense items as they occur each day and not have to open the software every day. Of course, it you want to, you can record these amounts on your computer as often as you like.

This Data Gathering Form must be completed before you can use them as the Starting Budget amounts for the next month.

If you don't do the data gathering and recording correctly and completely, you are not managing your budget properly.

Open the Data Gathering Form from the Monthly Budget Worksheet by clicking on the Enter Actual Income and Expense button.

The completed Data Gathering Form for income will look something like this:

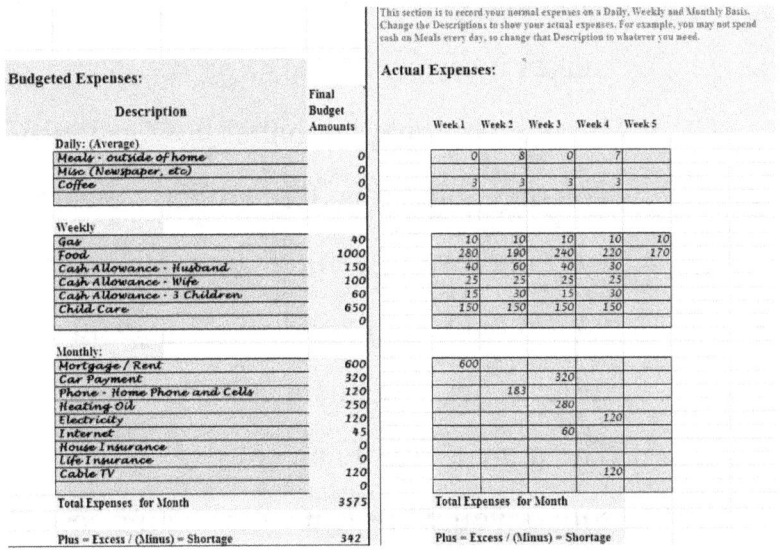

The completed Data Gathering Form for expenses
will look something like this:

Budgeting and Money Management - The Basics

Here are some points to consider when collecting and inputting your actual income and expense amounts.

1. Gather and input them as often as possible so you don't have all the input to do at the end of the month.

2. Ask your family members to get receipts for everything they buy with their monthly cash so you can input their actual expenses.

3. Don't worry about the pennies. Actually, rounding everything to the nearest dollar makes it easier.

4. Input everything no matter how insignificant you may think it is. Remember, you are working toward getting complete control of your money so if you leave things out it won't reflect your true financial condition.

5. The more diligent and consistent you are, the sooner you will see results and the sooner you

will be ready to start investing your extra money at the end of each month.

When you finish entering whatever income or expense amounts you have, click on the Go Back to Budget button to return to the Monthly Budget Worksheet.

You can go into and out of the Data Gathering Form as many times as you need to complete entering all the income and expense items for the month.

WHAT TO DO WITH THE BUDGET EXCESS OR SHORTAGE

After your budget is complete for the month and you have entered all your actual income and expense items, there will be either a budget shortage (you spent more than you earned) or a budget excess (you earned more than you spent). Of course, you should be striving to always have a budget excess.

As part of getting your money under control, you must define a plan to deal with the shortage or excess.

The Budget Summary Report will point you in the right direction to help with this plan.

Print the Budget Summary:

On the Main Menu:

Click Budget Summary

Click Print Budget Summary

The Budget Summary will look something like this:

Budgeting and Money Management - The Basics

Budget Summary and Actions to take to balance your budget: November   2014

Budget		Actual		Positive or Negative	Status
Income	3917	Income	2861	-1056	**Review Income Sources**
Expenses	3575	Expenses	3820	-245	**Review Expenses**
Total	342	Total	-959	-1301	**Complete Shortage Planning Form**

Proposed Actions to balance budget:

Actual Income is Less than Budgeted - Problem
          Income Action: **Review possible sources of extra Income**

Actual Expenses are more than Budgeted - Problem
          Expense Action: **Review all your expenses and make decisions where to reduce your expenses**

A Budget Shortage exists of   **-$1,301**
          Budget Action: **Complete the Budget Shortage Planning Form and take action on proposed steps**

This report shows the summary of your budget results for the month just completed.

Take a close look at this report.

It shows the total amounts you budgeted for Income and Expense and the Total (net difference) between the two figures.

It also shows the same information for your Actual Income and Expense as entered by you during the month.

Budgeting and Money Management - The Basics

The Positive or Negative column indicates whether your actual amounts were favorable or unfavorable for the month.

Finally, it gives some suggestions as to what to do to help bring your budget into balance.

One of the suggestions will be to complete either the Budget Shortage Form (as shown in the example) or the Budget Excess Planning Form.

Here is a sample of the Budget Shortage Planning Form. Use this if your expenses were more than your income for the month.

Budget Shortage Planning Form November 2014

This form can be used for 2 different purposes:
1. to help you plan for any budget shortage based on your completed budget for the month.
2. to test the impact of proposed changes to your budget before you actually make the changes.

Your Budget was short the following amount based on actual income and expense entered: -$1,301 Budget Shortage

My Plan to Cut Expenses and/or Increase Income to Balance Budget:

List below how you will balance your budget.

Income Options:	Estimated Amount **	Monthly Amount	Check as each is Completed
Work Overtime	w	0	
Get second job	w	0	
Get loan	w	0	
Borrow from family	1000 m	1000	
Other	w	0	
Total Additional Income Possible		1000	
Expense Options:	Est Savings		
Stop eating out / take lunch to work	5 d	110	
Take coffee from home	3 d	66	
Carpool to save gas expense	15 w	65	
Clip coupons for food purchases	20 w	87	
	d	0	
Total Decrease in Expenses Possible		328	
Continue until remaining balance is greater than shortage		1328	
Budget will be okay with these changes	Excess Now Exists	27	

59

As you enter information into the Income Options or the Expense Options areas, the software will adjust the figure on the bottom until the message "Excess Now Exists" appears. This means that you have made sufficient plans to deal with the budget shortage.

Notice the message "Budget will be okay with these changes". This simply means that you have temporarily taken care of your budget shortage problem. It obviously doesn't mean that all your problems are over.

Remember that another way to address this shortage is to do the detail review of your income and expense items as shown in other chapters if you opted not to do it at that time.

If there had been an excess in the budget for the month (your income was more than your expenses), the Budget Summary would look something like this.

Budget Summary and Actions to take to balance your budget: November   2014

Budget		Actual		Positive or Negative	Status
Income	3917	Income	5664	1747	**OKAY**
Expenses	3575	Expenses	3820	-245	**Review Expenses**
Total	342	Total	1844	1502	**Complete Excess Planning Form**

Proposed Actions to balance budget:

Actual Income is more than Budgeted - OKAY
    Income Action: Actual Income is More than Budgeted - You're Okay

Actual Expenses are more than Budgeted - Problem
    Expense Action: Review all your expenses and make decisions where to reduce your expenses

A Budget Excess Exists of $1,502
    Budget Action: Complete the Budget Excess Planning Form and take action on proposed steps

If, instead of that shortage, there was an excess in the budget at month end, completion of the Budget Excess Planning Form would be suggested. That Budget Excess Planning Form would look like this.

Budget Excess Planning Form   November   2014

This is to help you plan what to do with any excess money based on your completed budget for the month.

You have the following excess money available $1,502 Extra money available

This is how I Plan to Use the Extra Available Cash from the Budget:

	Amount	Check as each is Completed
List below what you will do with this excess money.		
1 Leave in Budget Management Account for use next month	100	
2 Deposit in Emergency Fund (you should strive for at least 6 months of net income in the Emergency Fund)	750	
3 Use for the following:		
Fix the Patio	150	
4 Use for Debt Reduction		
Mortgage partial extra payment	500	
5 Invest - list where you will invest		
6 Deposit in Goals Account		
Amount remaining to be allocated. Continue until this amount is zero	2	

So, regardless of whether you have an excess or a shortage at the end of the month, you must formalize your plan to deal with it. The Budget Summary, Budget Excess Planning Form and the Budget Shortage Planning Form are designed to make this step simpler and to help you keep your Money Action Plan on target.

Let's take a minute and review the different options for your excess money. As you can see, you have many possible places to put the extra money your budget has identified.

1. Budget Management. When you're just getting started, you may want to just leave the extra money in your Budget Management Account to be available for the next month if there is a shortage. This is probably the best option until you know that you will not need the money to help balance the next month's budget.

2. Emergency Fund. If you don't already have an Emergency Fund, then this is the next place you should put extra money. You should work on getting your Emergency Fund up to six times your regular monthly take home pay or six times your regular monthly bills, whichever is greater. So, if your regular monthly take home pay is $2500 and your bills are $2200, your Emergency Fund should have a balance of $15000. The Emergency

Fund is needed in case you lose your job or get injured and can't work. This fund will cover you and take care of your family for six months until you can get back to work.

3. Necessary Repairs. Use the extra money for repairs that <u>need</u> to be done. This does not mean building a deck just because you want one. It means such things as replacing your water heater if it has failed, fixing the car, etc. Again, things that <u>need</u> to be done not things you just want to do.

4. Debt Reduction. When you get to the point where you have extra money and you don't need it for Budget Management, Emergency Fund or necessary repairs, then this category, Debt Reduction, is the next area you should look at. See the Chapter "Reviewing Your Expenses" for some tips and ideas about this, which loans to pay off first and other ways to reduce your debt.

5. Investing. As a beginner, investing can be overwhelming. This topic is not specifically covered in this book but is discussed in depth in the third book in the Money Action Plan series: "Investing - The Basics". When you get to the point that you are ready to invest, the book is available online. It will help you get started in investing and give you some basic education about investing in stocks, bonds, and other investments.

6. Goals Account. Through the years, you will identify many financial goals that you want to accomplish. When you identify a goal, do the following:
    a. Estimate the total cost of the goal
    b. Estimate when you will need that total cost
    c. Divide this by the number of months until you need it

    d. Budget the monthly amount as a monthly expense on your budget.

    e. Each month , be sure to deposit that amount in your goals account.

It is possible to have more than one goal budgeted. Make sure you identify the goals on the budget and put the amounts budgeted away in a Goals Account each month.

ACCOUNTS NEEDED

A Word about the Accounts needed for the Money Action Plan;

There are several accounts that you need to properly use the Money Action Plan system. Here is a brief description of each.

Main Account – this is an account you can pay your bills from so it is usually a checking account. If you use online bill paying and are comfortable with it, continue to use it for this plan. Otherwise, writing checks works just as well.

Budget Management Account – this is an account where you accumulate your income for the month. While it can be the same account as your Main Account, the system works better if you use a separate account, such as a savings account. You must be able to get money out of the account at least four times each month so that when you are paying your bills each week, you can transfer money to the Main Account if needed.

Emergency Fund – This should be a separate account that is only used for the intended purpose, if you lose your job or are unable to work. Use a savings account for this.

Goals Account – This is an account for specific identified goals. Deposit the money identified on the budget for each goal into this account.

Investment and Retirement Accounts – these accounts are beyond the scope of this book. However, you may already have one or the other to use if you get to this point in your budgeting.

PREPARING FOR THE NEXT MONTH

After you have completed your budget for the month, you will want to prepare for the next month. The Money Action Plan system provides two buttons that will help you do that: Prepare All Reports and Prepare for Next Month.
These work as follows:

PREPARE ALL REPORTS

The Prepare All Reports button will print all the reports you will need for your records so that you don't have to go to each report and print it. Be sure that you have completed the following before you do this.

1. You need to input all the actual income and expense data for the month so that you have a record of it.

2. Second, you need to look at the Budget Summary Report and then complete either the Budget Excess Planning Report or the Budget Shortage Planning Report,

whichever is suggested by the Budget Summary Report.

3. Third, if you have any updates to Assets or Liabilities, enter the updates on the Asset List and the Liability List. This will update your Net-Worth Statement.

4. Finally, click on Prepare All Reports to print the following for your records:

> Monthly Budget Worksheet
>
> Data Gathering Form with Analysis
>
> Budget Summary
>
> Budget Excess Planning Form
>
> Budget Shortage Planning Form
>
> Net-Worth Statement (Includes Asset

List and Liability List after they have been entered).

PREPARE FOR NEXT MONTH
Now you are ready to prepare for the next month.

Click on the Prepare Next Month button. This will perform several actions.

1. Copies the actual income and expense amounts to the Budget Snapshot section of the Monthly Budget Worksheet. This lets you start your budget based on what actually happened in the previous month.

2. Clears the Data Gathering Form to get ready for the new month.

3. Clears the Budget Adjustment Section of the Monthly Budget Worksheet, both the explanations and amounts so you can start over inputting any necessary adjustments for the new month.

4. Changes the month to show the next month.

The Monthly Budget Worksheet will look like this after running the Prepare for Next Month.

Budgeting and Money Management - The Basics

Monthly Budget Worksheet

November - 2014

Budgeted Income: Description	Take Home	Code	Starting Budget Amounts	Adjusted Amount	Reason for Changing	Final Budget Amounts
Paycheck Take Home Amounts;		Help				
Husband check 1	212	m	212			212
Husband	95	m	95			95
Husband	270	m	270			270
Husband	250	m	250			250
Wife	120	m	120			120
Wife	487	m	487			487
Husband - 2nd Job	200	m	200			200
Husband - 2nd Job	197	m	197			197
Wife - babysitting	0	m	0			0
Wife - 2nd job	95	m	95			95
	0	m	0			0
	0	m	0			0
Other Income during Month:		Help				
Alimony	0	m	0			0
Child Support	285	m	285			285
Gifts	0	m	0			0
Sale of personal items	650	m	650			650
	0	m	0			0
Pay back	0	m	0			0
Total Spendable Income for Month	2861		2861			2861

Budget Snapshot / **Budget Adjustment**

Budgeted Expenses: Description	Amount	Code	Starting Budget Amounts	Adjusted Amount	Reason for Changing	Final Budget Amounts
Daily: (Average)		Help				
Meals - outside of home	15	m	15			15
Misc (Newspaper, etc)	0	m	0			0
Coffee	12	m	12			12
	0	m	0			0
Weekly		Help				
Gas	50	m	50			50
Food	1100	m	1100			1100
Cash Allowance - Husband	170	m	170			170
Cash Allowance - Wife	100	m	100			100
Cash Allowance - 3 Children	90	m	90			90
Child Care	600	m	600			600
	0	m	0			0
Monthly:		Help				
Mortgage / Rent	600	m	600			600
Car Payment	320	m	320			320
Phone - Home Phone and Cells	183	m	183			183
Heating Oil	280	m	280			280
Electricity	120	m	120			120
Internet	60	m	60			60
House Insurance	0	m	0			0
Life Insurance	0	m	0			0
Cable TV	120	m	120			120
	0	m	0			0
Total Expenses for Month	3820		3820			3820
Plus = Excess / (Minus) = Shortage			(959)			(959)

There are several things you should do immediately:

1. Delete anything that was a one-time income or expense such as the income item "Sale of Personal Items".

2. NOTE that all the codes are changed to "m" for monthly because it was monthly totals that were transferred.

3. You are able to change these codes to work however you want to create your budget, for instance, the ones in the daily and weekly sections of expenses, we suggest you change the amounts and then change the code back to "d" for daily or "w" for weekly. This gives you better insight into what is actually being spent so that you can make the necessary decisions about changes. It's entirely up to you which way is easier.

Then proceed with your normal budget preparation procedures by reviewing all the income and expense items and making Budget Adjustments to bring the total budget Excess or Shortage to a figure that is manageable for you.

Go back to <u>Create Your Budget Snapshot</u> to start the process over again. You may have to do this several months until you get totally familiarized with the process and it becomes second nature as to what you need to do.

The results will be worth it!

Budgeting and Money Management - The Basics

MANAGING THE PROCESS

DAILY ACTIVITIES

- To Maintain what is needed to keep your budget under control:
  - Keep track of all income items *including cash paid to you or any of your family members*. This is where a lot of budgets go wrong by not including cash received as part of the budget.
  - Keep track of all expenses paid. This has to include ALL expenses, even cash paid for coffee, lunch, newspaper, etc.

WEEKLY ACTIVITIES

- Pay Bills and transfer money from the Budget Management Account to the Main Account as necessary.
- Gather pay stubs and other proof of income received

- Record all income and payments for the week on the Data Gathering Form.
- This data will be used for the next monthly budget

MONTHLY ACTIVITIES

- Review the Budget Summary Report for information about what needs to be done to help bring your budget under control if there is still a budget shortage for the month.
- Complete either the Budget Shortage Form or the Budget Excess Form, whichever the Budget Summary Form suggests.
- Whatever you decide on the Budget Shortage or Budget Excess Forms, be sure that these decisions are reflected in your next budget.
- Prepare your Starting Budget amounts for the following month by transferring actual income and expense amounts for the month to the Starting Budget Amounts. The Money Action Plan software will do this for you by

clicking on the "Prepare for Next Month" button.

- Review your assets and update the valuations of each
- Review your liabilities and update the balances of each
- Create your Net-Worth Statement to see progress. The Net-Worth Statement will be used to measure your month to month progress on your Money Action Plan. HOWEVER, the Net-Worth Statement cannot be created until you perform the List Your Assets and List Your Liabilities steps in the plan. See List Your Assets and List Your Liabilities chapters for the details of how to perform these steps.
- Print All Reports for the month

YEARLY ACTIVITIES

After you complete your final budget for the year,

- Print All Reports to retain for your records.

- Consider starting from scratch for the New Year. The software will role over the end of year actual income and expense amounts for you to start the new year but sometimes it's better to start over with the Budget Snapshot, Review of Income and Expenses, etc.
- Remember, nothing is stopping you from conducting a review of your income and expenses at any time.
- Review the progress you made through the year and make any adjustments to the way you budget so you can accomplish even more in the coming year
- DON'T GIVE UP! Sometimes a lack of significant progress can cause some disillusionment with the process. But look back on the year and realize everything you have learned and look forward to better progress in the new year. You have laid the

groundwork for getting to retirement in comfort.

Budgeting and Money Management - The Basics

REVIEW AND MAXIMIZE YOUR INCOME

PREPARATION

- Complete your Budget Snapshot
- Have your pay stubs and evidence of other income available for the review process

REVIEW EACH INCOME ITEM

Objective:

Maximize your take home pay to make more money available for paying your expenses.

To accomplish the objective, you need to review each item listed on your Budget Snapshot and make decisions about each one.

Reviewing your income actually consists of two parts;

- Review the money you actually take home and try to maximize it

- Review all your payroll deductions that reduce the money you take home and try to minimize them.

There is much more detail about this step and information about how to review your income in the second book in the Money Action Plan Series titled "Keep More of What You Earn". You don't necessarily need that book but, as I said, I have included a lot of detail about the review process.

NOTE: Sometimes you won't know how much your take home pay will change based on changes that you make until you receive your next paycheck. Don't go change your Final Budget amounts to reflect these changes.

Let me make this perfectly clear:
NEVER go back and change your Final Budget amounts. This defeats the purpose of budgeting in the first place.

Instead, just enter the amounts received or paid in the Data Gathering Section and adjust the Starting Budget amounts in the following month.

Budgeting and Money Management - The Basics

Example of budget changes on Budget Worksheet:

Income Changes Example:

Monthly Budget Worksheet *Sample Form*			Budget Snapshot		Budget Adjustment		
November 2014				Starting Budget Amounts	Adjust Amount To:	Reason for Changing	Final Budget Amounts
Budgeted Income: Description	Take Home	Code					
Paycheck Take Home Amounts;		*Help*					
Husband check 1	310	*o*		335	350	*Change W4*	350
Husband	350	*o*		378			378
Husband	310	*o*		335			335
Husband	350	*o*		378			378
Wife	240	*t*		521			521
Wife	170	*t*		369			369
Husband - 2nd Job	80	*t*		174			174
Husband - 2nd Job	70	*t*		152			152
Wife - babysitting	80	*m*		80			80
Wife - 2nd job	130	*m*		130	0	*Company closed*	0
		m		0			0
		m		0			0
Other Income during Month:		*Help*					
Alimony		*m*		0			0
Child Support	110	*w*		476	380	*Received advance l...*	380
Gifts		*m*		0			0
Sale of personal items		*m*		0	800	*Sell Snowmobile*	800
		m		0			0
		m		0			0
Total Spendable Income for Month				3328			3917

As you make these changes, the software will recalculate the Final Budget Amount based on the new amount you input in the Adjusted Amount column. Your Final Budget will be ready after any adjustments are also made in Expense areas as explained in the next chapter.

REVIEW AND MINIMIZE YOUR EXPENSES

PREPARATION

- Complete your Budget Snapshot
- Have evidence of all your bills paid including amounts family members use for daily expenses and bills paid in cash. Any money going out should be considered a bill.
- Have evidence of any money paid out in cash.

There is much more detail about this step and information about how to review your expenses in the second book in the Money Action Plan Series titled "Keep More of What You Earn". You don't necessarily need that book but, as I said, I have included a lot of detail about the review process.

Budgeting and Money Management - The Basics

REVIEW YOUR EXPENSES
Objective:

Minimize your monthly expense payments without compromising your Money Action Plan. By this I mean that you need to be smart about lowering your expenses. For instance, don't pay only the minimum on your credit cards just to minimize your monthly expenses. Because credit card debt is a very high interest debt, you want to pay it off as quickly as possible.

To accomplish this objective, you need to review each expense item listed on your Budget Snapshot and make decisions about each one.

Reviewing your expense is a little more difficult than the review you just completed of your income sources. There are two parts to the review;

- Review the money you actually pay out each month and try to minimize it

- Review ways to reduce or manage what you have more efficiently and quickly pay down or pay off debt.

Expense Changes Example:

Monthly Budget Worksheet *Sample Form*

November   2014 | Budget Snapshot | **Budget Adjustment**

NOTE: The Daily, Weekly and Monthly Sections are for illustration purposes only. The real software does not have these. You use the Code to indicate how often the expense occurs.

Budgeted Expenses: Description	Amount	Code	Starting Budget Amounts	Budget Adjustment Adjust Amount To:	Reason for Changing	Final Budget Amounts
Daily: (Average)		Help				
Meals - outside of home	6	d	180	0	Take lunch	0
Misc (Newspaper, etc)	1	d	30	0	Read at office	0
Coffee	2	d	60	0	Get coffee at office	0
		d	0			0
		d	0			0
		d	0			0
		d	0			0
Weekly		Help				
Gas	40	w	173	40	Car pool	40
Food	300	w	1299	1000	Coupons	1000
Cash Allowance - Husband	50	w	217	150	Reduce allowance	150
Cash Allowance - Wife	50	w	217	100	Reduce allowance	100
Cash Allowance - 3 Children	45	w	195	60	Reduce allowance	60
Child Care	150	w	650			650
		w	0			0
		w	0			0
		w	0			0
		w	0			0
		w	0			0
		w	0			0
Monthly:		Help				
Mortgage / Rent	600	m	600			600
Car Payment	320	m	320			320
Phone - Home Phone and Cells	200	m	200	120	Change plan	120
Heating Oil	300	m	300	250	Reduce thermostat	250
Electricity	140	m	140	120	Turn off lights, tvs,	120
Internet	60	m	60	45	Change plan	45
House Insurance	450	m	450	0	Not due this month	0
Life Insurance	270	m	270	0	Cancel Insurance	0
Cable TV	120	m	120			120
		m	0			0
		m	0			0
		m	0			0
Total Expenses for Month			5981			3575
Plus = Excess / (Minus) = Shortage			(2153)			342

Budgeting and Money Management - The Basics

As you make these changes, the software will recalculate the Final Budget Amount based on the new amount you input in the Adjusted Amount column. Your Final Budget will then be ready as soon as this is done.

LIST YOUR ASSETS

Let's make sure we know the definition of an asset.

An Asset can be defined as anything that you own.

They are usually divided into at least the following

three categories:

- Liquid Assets - these are sometimes called cash assets
    - Examples:
        - Balance of Checking Account
        - Balance of Savings Accounts (Budget Management Account, Goals Account, Emergency Fund)
        - Cash you have in your pocket or in the home
- Non-liquid Assets - these are other investments that you have that are not cash and cannot be converted to cash quickly
    - Examples
        - Your home (the current value)
        - Investments in Stocks, Bonds, Mutual Funds
        - Cars (the current value)

- Snowmobiles, Skidoos, ATVs, etc
- Collections (coins, baseball cards, art, etc)
- Personal Property - these are assets that you use in your daily life that you are not holding for investment purposes
  - Examples:
    - Clothes
    - Furniture
    - Other home furnishings
    - Jewelry

Just because your asset is not listed doesn't mean it is not your asset List the value of anything you own. **There are NO Exceptions!**

PREPARATION FOR LISTING YOUR ASSETS

There are 3 steps to prepare for listing your assets. They are as follows:

- List what you think are your assets based on the list above

- Gather all the information you have about the assets you listed
- Spend some time determining the current value of those assets you have listed

HOW TO FIND VALUES FOR YOUR ASSETS

You may be wondering or confused about how you determine what some of your assets are worth. Here are some ideas.

Home

There are a couple of ways to determine what your home may be worth on the current market. Websites like www.zillow.com can give you an idea of the value of your home. I use this because it's easy to look it up whenever you need it. But I really only change this value every six months because the changes on a monthly basis are usually too small to worry about. To do this, just go to the site, put in your address and look at the Zestimate for your property.

You can also ask a realtor to do a sales comparable analysis for your home to determine what its worth. This takes more time and is difficult to do every six months or every year to update your asset values.

Cars

Car values can be estimated by going to the Kelly Blue Book site, http://www.kbb.com. Just go to the site, enter the information about your car and it will give you a current value for your car.

Investments (Stocks, Bonds, Mutual Funds, 401K Accounts, IRA Accounts, etc)

The value of any of your investments can usually be found online of in a monthly statement. If you don't have access to your investments online, you should find out how to do this by asking someone who may know. If you are looking for the value of an employer retirement or investment account, ask your employer for instructions about how to look at your account online.

If you have your own account, check with the investment company about getting monthly statements and about seeing your investments online.

Checking and Savings Accounts

For your checking and savings accounts, check with the bank they are with to make sure you get statements or can see these online.

Snowmobiles, Skidoos, ATVs, motorcycles, etc

These items can also be found on the Kelly Blue Book site.

Use the following links:

For snowmobiles: http://www.kbb.com/snowmobile

For motorcycles: http://www.kbb.com/motorcycles

For skidoos:

http://www.kbb.com/personalwatercraft

For ATVs: http://www.kbb.com/motorcycles/4-wheel-atv

Collections (coins, baseball cards, art, etc)

Personal collections are one of the most difficult items to place a value on.

The best you can do is to hire an expert in whatever the subject matter of the collection is and get a reasonably good estimate of the worth of this asset. I would probably not do this more often than once a year especially if I was paying for the appraisal. Once every two or three years would be fine as far as calculating your Net-Worth.

PERSONAL PROPERTY

Jewelry

Jewelry can be appraised by any reputable and qualified jeweler. As with collections above, this will only need to be done once a year or even less if you don't have very many jewelry items of any significant worth.

Clothes, Furniture, Other home

furnishings

It really isn't necessary to even include these in your asset list unless you have some items of considerable worth such as antiques. If so, these can be valued by any qualified antiques dealer.

IIow to List Your Assets

From the Main Menu of the Money Action Plan software, click on the Asset List.

In the Assets Section, list all the assets you identified above and the value of each.

By the way, your assets are one half of the information needed to calculate your Net-Worth. As soon as you complete the next chapter, List Your Liabilities, you will be able to calculate and review your Net-Worth.

So, let's move on and look at your liabilities.

Here is an example of what your list of assets should look like:

Budgeting and Money Management - The Basics

Assets

Cash

Main Checking Account	2000	
Budget Management Account	100	
Emergency Fund	100	
Goals Savings Account(s)	100	
Total Cash		2300

Personal Assets

Main House	125000	
Second or Vacation Home		
Auto - Minivan	8000	
Auto 2 - Ford Pickup	5500	
	100	
	100	
	100	
Total Personal Assets		138800

Collections / Valuables

Jewelry	100	
Art	100	
Total Valuables		200

Investments

Savings Bonds	100	
Certificates of Deposit	1500	
Mutual Funds		
Stocks		
Bonds		
Total Investments		1600

Retirement Funds

IRA, Traditional	15000	
IRA, Ross	20000	
401K, 403B, 457	13000	
Employer Pension		
Total Retirement Assets		48000

Total Assets	190900

Budgeting and Money Management - The Basics

LIST YOUR LIABILITIES

First, let's discuss what a liability is as compared to any other monthly expense that you pay.

For your budgeting purposes, a liability can be defined as something that you owe that will not be paid off within the month that you are budgeting. This means that if you have a Mortgage on your house, for instance, the total amount of what you owe on the mortgage at the time that you list your liabilities is your Mortgage Liability.

The amount you pay monthly for the mortgage is your monthly mortgage expense and that should have been listed under expenses in the Budget Snapshot section on your Monthly Budget Worksheet.

Here is a list of items that may be Liabilities.

Mortgage balance including second mortgages

Car Loan balance

Other loan balances

Student Loans

Home Improvement Loans

Consumer Loans (for electronics (Tvs,
computers, etc), furniture, lawn
equipment, etc

Balance owed for back taxes that are
being paid in installments

Balance owed for medical, dental or eye
doctors.

NOTE: Just because your loan is not listed doesn't
mean it is not your liability. List the balances on
anything you owe. **There are NO Exceptions!**

PREPARATION FOR LISTING YOUR LIABILITIES
There are 3 steps to prepare for listing your
liabilities. They are as follows:

- List what you think are your liabilities based
  on the list above

- Gather all the information you have about the
  liabilities you listed

- Spend some time determining the current balance owed on the liability that you have listed either from statements or by going online.

HOW TO FIND VALUES FOR YOUR LIABILITIES
Determining the value of your liabilities is usually a lot simpler than it was for your assets. You should have some kind of a statement for most of the balances that you owe. The amount you owe is usually shown as the Current Balance.

HOW TO LIST YOUR LIABILITIES
From the Main Menu of the Money Action Plan software, click on the Liability List.

In the Liabilities Section, list all the debt that you have and the current balance owed on each of them.

Here is an example of what your list of liabilities should look like:

Liabilities

Short Term (less than 1 year)

Visa Balance	800
Master Card Balance	500
American Express Balance	1200
Discover Balance	
Education Loan 1 - Balance	13000
Education Loan 2 - Balance	
Furniture Loan Balance	400
Electronics Loan Balance	
Mattress Loan Balance	
HSNetwork, etc Balance	
Total Short Term Liabilities	**15900**

Long Term (over 1 year)

Mortgage Balance	92000
Second Mortgage Balance	
	4400
	3000
Total Long Term Liabilities	**99400**

Total Liabilities   **115300**

Your Liabilities are the second half of your Net-Worth. Once you have completed the Liabilities section, notice that your Net-Worth is displayed just below the liabilities list.

So, let's take a look at the Net-Worth Statement and what it means to you as part of your MONEY

ACTION PLAN.

PREPARE YOUR NET-WORTH STATEMENT

As you saw, the Net-Worth Statement was automatically prepared as you entered your Asset List and your Liability List.

Click on the "Print Net-Worth Statement" button to print the report.

The whole Net-Worth Statement will look like this.

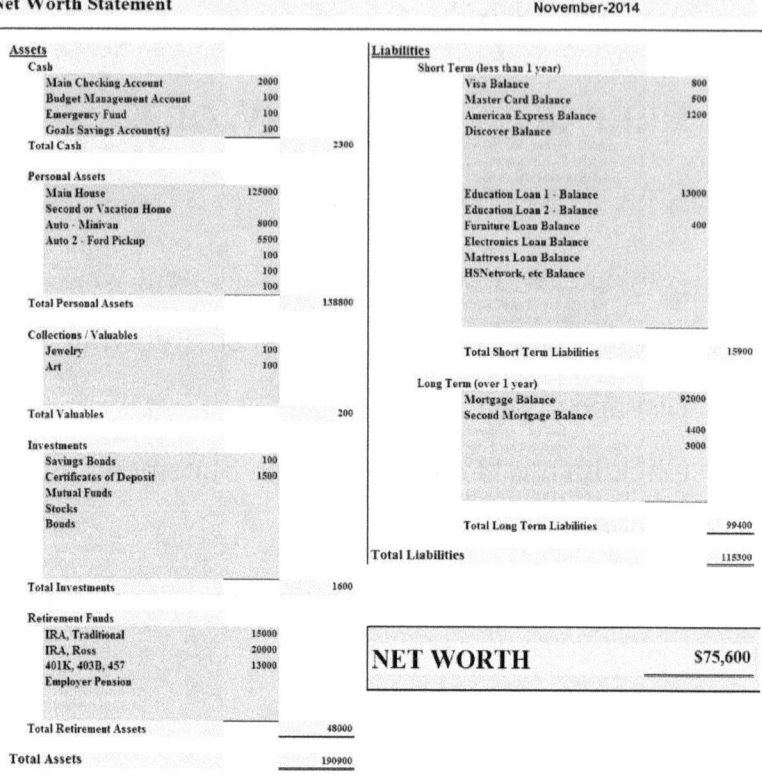

Net Worth Statement   November-2014

Assets				Liabilities		
Cash				**Short Term (less than 1 year)**		
Main Checking Account	2000			Visa Balance	800	
Budget Management Account	100			Master Card Balance	500	
Emergency Fund	100			American Express Balance	1200	
Goals Savings Account(s)	100			Discover Balance		
Total Cash		2300				
Personal Assets						
Main House	125000			Education Loan 1 - Balance	13000	
Second or Vacation Home				Education Loan 2 - Balance		
Auto - Minivan	8000			Furniture Loan Balance	400	
Auto 2 - Ford Pickup	5500			Electronics Loan Balance		
	100			Mattress Loan Balance		
	100			HSNetwork, etc Balance		
	100					
Total Personal Assets		138800				
Collections / Valuables						
Jewelry	100			Total Short Term Liabilities		15900
Art	100					
				Long Term (over 1 year)		
				Mortgage Balance	92000	
Total Valuables		200		Second Mortgage Balance		
					4400	
Investments					3000	
Savings Bonds	100					
Certificates of Deposit	1500					
Mutual Funds						
Stocks						
Bonds				Total Long Term Liabilities		99400
				Total Liabilities		115300
Total Investments		1600				
Retirement Funds						
IRA, Traditional	15000					
IRA, Ross	20000					
401K, 403B, 457	13000			**NET WORTH**		**$75,600**
Employer Pension						
Total Retirement Assets		48000				
Total Assets		190900				

You've probably determined by now that your Net-Worth is nothing more than the difference between what you own (Assets) and what you owe (Liabilities). There is no mystery to this.

You should review your Net-Worth to determine whether you are making progress on your MONEY ACTION PLAN. Your Net-Worth should slowly rise over the course of your life to show that you are progressing in your long term goals to manage your money.

A note of caution however is needed. Your Net-Worth may go down slightly during any given month based on what you do. For instance, if you spend some money without gaining an asset to list on the Asset List (such as paying for college), this will cause your Net-Worth to decrease temporarily. Don't be too alarmed by this.

The increase in Net-Worth should be a long term goal, over the course of years, not necessarily measured month by month. The main reason for looking at it on a monthly basis is to keep track of it so you don't loose control.

REVIEW AND PREPARATION FOR CREATING YOUR NET-WORTH STATEMENT EACH MONTH

REVIEW YOUR ASSETS AND THE VALUATIONS OF EACH

REVIEW YOUR LIABILITIES AND THE BALANCES OF EACH

PREPARE YOUR NET-WORTH STATEMENT (AS YOU HAVE SEEN, THE SOFTWARE WILL DO THIS FOR YOU)

BONUS MATERIAL

To prepare you for going further into the Money Action Plan process, I have included the following bonus material. This Money Management Diagram, will give you some information about the entire plan which eventually includes investments, retirement planning and estate planning.

MONEY MANAGEMENT DIAGRAM

This diagram represents the entire Money Action Plan process including subjects that are not covered in this book; i.e. Investments, Retirement Accounts, Short and Long Term Goals and Estate Planning. These are additional books in the Money Action Plan Series. Publication dates for these can be found on the website moneyactionplan.com. Also, this diagram can be printed from the website.

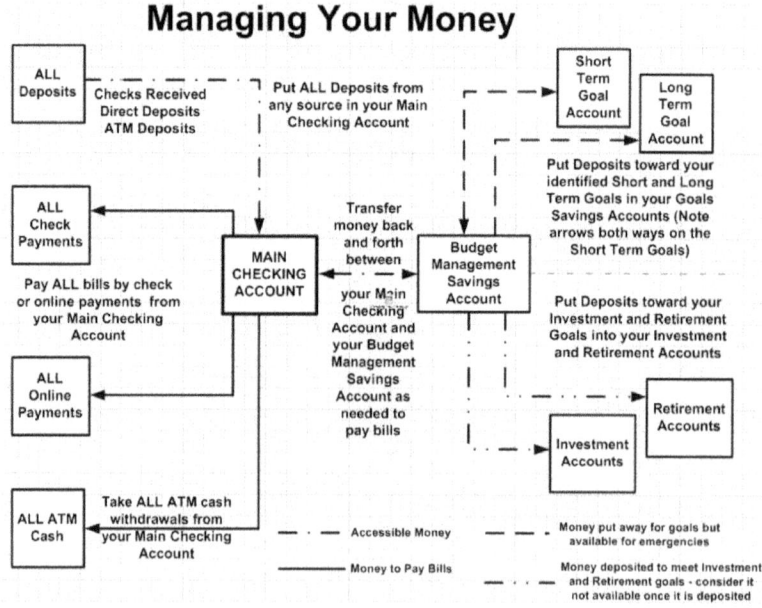

Managing Your Money

Let me explain the details of this diagram.

Accounts Needed

The **Main Account** can be either a checking or a savings account. A checking account is best because you will be paying all bills out of this account.

Rules for the Main Account

All Payments come from this account– no exceptions

Includes ALL expenses paid for any purpose or by any method (check, atm, automatic payment, etc)

There are no exceptions

The **Budget Management Account** should be an account that earns interest and is easily accessible for transfers in and out. As of this writing it is difficult to get very much interest on a savings account but believe me when I say that anything is better than nothing. Some savings accounts limit the number of transfers out that can be done each month so make sure that yours allows at least 5 transfers out each month just in case you need money from the account each week. This is because you will be managing your budget on a weekly basis and may need to transfer money from the Budget Management Account to the Main Account each week.

Rules for the Budget Management Account

- All Deposits go into this account – no exceptions
- Includes ALL income from any source
- ***There are no exceptions***; all payroll deposits, cash received from anywhere for any purpose, checks received for any purpose

The **Short Term and Long Term Goal Account** is used for saving money for identified future goals (buying a car, down payment for house, etc). It is usually a savings account. This account is not needed and should not be used until your monthly budget is under control.

Goals Accounts

- For identified Short Term goals

- For identified long term goals
- Goals should be identified with the total amount needed, the goal date, how much is needed weekly or monthly to meet goal

The **Investment / Retirements Accounts** will be needed as you progress toward making investments and retirement deposits. If you are just working on getting your budget under control, don't be concerned with these accounts. They will be explained as needed.

Rules for Transfers between accounts:

Main Account to/from Budget Management Account

- Weekly transfers as necessary based on a review of upcoming expenses
- Monthly transfers as needed between accounts based on monthly budget review

Budget Management Account to/from Short or Long Term Goal Account, Investment Account(s), Retirement Account(s)

- Transfers only based on budget decisions. Remember that money transferred to the Goals Accounts, Investment Accounts and Retirement Accounts should be considered as off limits for your regular budget activity, paying your monthly bills.

ABOUT THE AUTHOR

Neil Bryan spent the first part of his career in the banking business, working for many years as a teller, loan clerk, programmer, and computer operator and eventually as an auditor and an Electronic Data Processing (EDP) Auditor at various banks in New England and Florida. Eventually he quit the working world to start his own business selling and installing small business computer systems and software, designing systems and teaching.

While trying to make a go of the business, he got into teaching at the community college level; courses in computer science, programming, systems analysis.

While doing this he decided to finish his education by completing his Bachelor's degree in Business Administration and his Master's in Business

Administration (MBA) and went into the field of business systems consulting work, working on various large scale projects throughout the U.S and also in Japan.

During the time he was working on his Bachelor's degree, he and his wife decided to put together a plan for budgeting and managing their money. The result is this Money Action Plan system software and the accompanying book "Budgeting and Money Management – The Basics". They have been using this plan for almost thirty years.

Now that he is retired, in addition to documenting the Money Action Plan in the book and software, he is now working on additional books in the series (Keep More of What You Earn, Investing – The Basics, Retirement Planning – The Basics, Estate Planning – The Basics). He is also currently managing the website forum and blog at www.moneyactionplan.com. In addition, he is available to teach Money Action Plan seminars.

To contact him with questions or comments or to book a speaking engagement regarding personal finance or the complete seven-step Money Action Plan Seminar; use the Comment/Inquiry form on the website at www.moneyactionplan.com.

Budgeting and Money Management - The Basics

CONTINUE THE JOURNEY TO YOUR OWN COMPLETE MONEY ACTION PLAN

If you enjoyed this book and software, you can take the next step in your Money Action Plan with the next book in the series:

Keep More of What You Earn: Book 2 of the Money Action Plan Series. This book provides all the details of how to review and maximize your income and how to review and minimize your expenses. It also includes a year's worth of forms for creating a manual budget.

Other Books in the Money Action Plan Series
Investing - The Basics: Book 3 of the Money Action Plan Series.
This book is currently in the works.

Budgeting and Money Management - The Basics

Retirement Planning - The Basics: Book 4 of the Money Action Plan Series

Estate Planning - The Basics: Book 5 of the Money Action Plan Series

For information about when each of these will be available, go to www.moneyaction plan.com. Announcements of the book publishing dates will be available on the website.

OTHER BOOKS BY NEIL BRYAN

<u>My Everyday Everything Planning Book</u>

Plan anything you need or want to do.

<u>Rental Property Records Book</u>

Keep all your annual records for up to 12 rental properties in one book

MANUAL INCOME AND EXPENSE REVIEW FORMS

Use these forms for listing your income and expenses in preparation for entering them into the Money Action Plan software.

You can also use these forms as your budget if you don't have a computer or can't run the software.

Budgeting and Money Management - The Basics

Budgeting and Money Management - The Basics

Monthly Budget Worksheet - Budget Snapshot		**Month:**			
Budgeted Income:		**Budget Adjustment**			
	A	**B**	**C**		**D**
Description	Monthly Take Home Amounts	Adjust Amount To:	Reason for Changing		Final Budget Amounts
1					
2					
3					
4					
5					
6					
Other Income:					
7					
8					
9					
10					
11 Total Spendable Income for Month (Add 1-10)					
Budgeted Expenses:		**Budget Adjustment**			
Description	Monthly Amount	Adjust Amount To:	Reason for Changing		Final Budget Amounts
12					
13					
14					
15					
16					
17					
18					
19					
20					
21					
22					
23					
24					
25					
26					
27					
28					
29					
30					
31					
32					
33					
34					
35					
36					
37					
38					
39					
40					
41					
42					
43					
44					
45					
46					
47 Total Expenses for Month (Add 12 - 46)					
48 Plus = Excess / (Minus) = Shortage (11 minus 47)					

Budgeting and Money Management - The Basics

Budgeting and Money Management - The Basics

	Monthly Budget Worksheet - Budget Snapshot	**Month:**			
	Budgeted Income:		**Budget Adjustment**		
		A	**B**	**C**	**D**
	Description	Monthly Take Home Amounts	Adjust Amount To:	Reason for Changing	Final Budget Amounts
1					
2					
3					
4					
5					
6					
	Other Income:				
7					
8					
9					
10					
11	Total Spendable Income for Month (Add 1-10)				
	Budgeted Expenses:		**Budget Adjustment**		
	Description	Monthly Amount	Adjust Amount To:	Reason for Changing	Final Budget Amounts
12					
13					
14					
15					
16					
17					
18					
19					
20					
21					
22					
23					
24					
25					
26					
27					
28					
29					
30					
31					
32					
33					
34					
35					
36					
37					
38					
39					
40					
41					
42					
43					
44					
45					
46					
47	Total Expenses for Month (Add 12 - 46)				
48	Plus = Excess / (Minus) = Shortage (11 minus 47)				

Budgeting and Money Management - The Basics

Monthly Budget Worksheet - Budget Snapshot	**Month:**			
Budgeted Income:	**Budget Adjustment**			
	A	**B**	**C**	**D**
Description	Monthly Take Home Amounts	Adjust Amount To:	Reason for Changing	Final Budget Amounts
1				
2				
3				
4				
5				
6				
Other Income:				
7				
8				
9				
10				
11 Total Spendable Income for Month (Add 1-10)				
Budgeted Expenses:	**Budget Adjustment**			
Description	Monthly Amount	Adjust Amount To:	Reason for Changing	Final Budget Amounts
12				
13				
14				
15				
16				
17				
18				
19				
20				
21				
22				
23				
24				
25				
26				
27				
28				
29				
30				
31				
32				
33				
34				
35				
36				
37				
38				
39				
40				
41				
42				
43				
44				
45				
46				
47 Total Expenses for Month (Add 12 - 46)				
48 Plus = Excess / (Minus) = Shortage (11 minus 47)				

Budgeting and Money Management - The Basics

Monthly Budget Worksheet - Budget Snapshot		**Month:**			
Budgeted Income:		**Budget Adjustment**			
	A	**B**	**C**		**D**
Description	Monthly Take Home Amounts	Adjust Amount To:	Reason for Changing		Final Budget Amounts
1					
2					
3					
4					
5					
6					
Other Income:					
7					
8					
9					
10					
11 Total Spendable Income for Month (Add 1-10)					
Budgeted Expenses:		**Budget Adjustment**			
Description	Monthly Amount	Adjust Amount To:	Reason for Changing		Final Budget Amounts
12					
13					
14					
15					
16					
17					
18					
19					
20					
21					
22					
23					
24					
25					
26					
27					
28					
29					
30					
31					
32					
33					
34					
35					
36					
37					
38					
39					
40					
41					
42					
43					
44					
45					
46					
47 Total Expenses for Month (Add 12 - 46)					
48 Plus = Excess / (Minus) = Shortage (11 minus 47)					

Budgeting and Money Management - The Basics

Budgeting and Money Management - The Basics

Monthly Budget Worksheet - Budget Snapshot		**Month:**		
Budgeted Income:		**Budget Adjustment**		
	A	**B**	**C**	**D**
Description	Monthly Take Home Amounts	Adjust Amount To:	Reason for Changing	Final Budget Amounts
1				
2				
3				
4				
5				
6				
Other Income:				
7				
8				
9				
10				
11 Total Spendable Income for Month (Add 1-10)				
Budgeted Expenses:		**Budget Adjustment**		
Description	Monthly Amount	Adjust Amount To:	Reason for Changing	Final Budget Amounts
12				
13				
14				
15				
16				
17				
18				
19				
20				
21				
22				
23				
24				
25				
26				
27				
28				
29				
30				
31				
32				
33				
34				
35				
36				
37				
38				
39				
40				
41				
42				
43				
44				
45				
46				
47 Total Expenses for Month (Add 12 - 46)				
48 Plus = Excess / (Minus) = Shortage (11 minus 47)				

Budgeting and Money Management - The Basics

Monthly Budget Worksheet - Budget Snapshot	**Month:**			
Budgeted Income:		**Budget Adjustment**		
	A	**B**	**C**	**D**
Description	Monthly Take Home Amounts	Adjust Amount To:	Reason for Changing	Final Budget Amounts
1				
2				
3				
4				
5				
6				
Other Income:				
7				
8				
9				
10				
11 Total Spendable Income for Month (Add 1-10)				
Budgeted Expenses:		**Budget Adjustment**		
Description	Monthly Amount	Adjust Amount To:	Reason for Changing	Final Budget Amounts
12				
13				
14				
15				
16				
17				
18				
19				
20				
21				
22				
23				
24				
25				
26				
27				
28				
29				
30				
31				
32				
33				
34				
35				
36				
37				
38				
39				
40				
41				
42				
43				
44				
45				
46				
47 Total Expenses for Month (Add 12 - 46)				
48 Plus = Excess / (Minus) = Shortage (11 minus 47)				

Budgeting and Money Management - The Basics

Monthly Budget Worksheet - Budget Snapshot		**Month:**		
Budgeted Income:		**Budget Adjustment**		
	A	**B**	**C**	**D**
Description	Monthly Take Home Amounts	Adjust Amount To:	Reason for Changing	Final Budget Amounts
1				
2				
3				
4				
5				
6				
Other Income:				
7				
8				
9				
10				
11 Total Spendable Income for Month (Add 1-10)				
Budgeted Expenses:		**Budget Adjustment**		
Description	Monthly Amount	Adjust Amount To:	Reason for Changing	Final Budget Amounts
12				
13				
14				
15				
16				
17				
18				
19				
20				
21				
22				
23				
24				
25				
26				
27				
28				
29				
30				
31				
32				
33				
34				
35				
36				
37				
38				
39				
40				
41				
42				
43				
44				
45				
46				
47 Total Expenses for Month (Add 12 - 46)				
48 Plus = Excess / (Minus) = Shortage (11 minus 47)				

Budgeting and Money Management - The Basics

Monthly Budget Worksheet - Budget Snapshot		**Month:**			
Budgeted Income:		**Budget Adjustment**			
	A	B	C		D
Description	Monthly Take Home Amounts	Adjust Amount To:	Reason for Changing		Final Budget Amounts
1					
2					
3					
4					
5					
6					
Other Income:					
7					
8					
9					
10					
11 Total Spendable Income for Month (Add 1-10)					
Budgeted Expenses:		**Budget Adjustment**			
Description	Monthly Amount	Adjust Amount To:	Reason for Changing		Final Budget Amounts
12					
13					
14					
15					
16					
17					
18					
19					
20					
21					
22					
23					
24					
25					
26					
27					
28					
29					
30					
31					
32					
33					
34					
35					
36					
37					
38					
39					
40					
41					
42					
43					
44					
45					
46					
47 Total Expenses for Month (Add 12 - 46)					
48 Plus = Excess / (Minus) = Shortage (11 minus 47)					

Budgeting and Money Management - The Basics

Budgeting and Money Management - The Basics

Monthly Budget Worksheet - Budget Snapshot				Month:	
Budgeted Income:		**Budget Adjustment**			
	A	**B**	**C**		**D**
Description	Monthly Take Home Amounts	Adjust Amount To:	Reason for Changing		Final Budget Amounts
1					
2					
3					
4					
5					
6					
Other Income:					
7					
8					
9					
10					
11 Total Spendable Income for Month (Add 1-10)					
Budgeted Expenses:		**Budget Adjustment**			
Description	Monthly Amount	Adjust Amount To:	Reason for Changing		Final Budget Amounts
12					
13					
14					
15					
16					
17					
18					
19					
20					
21					
22					
23					
24					
25					
26					
27					
28					
29					
30					
31					
32					
33					
34					
35					
36					
37					
38					
39					
40					
41					
42					
43					
44					
45					
46					
47 Total Expenses for Month (Add 12 - 46)					
48 Plus = Excess / (Minus) = Shortage (11 minus 47)					

Budgeting and Money Management - The Basics

Budgeting and Money Management - The Basics

Monthly Budget Worksheet - Budget Snapshot	**Month:**			
Budgeted Income:		**Budget Adjustment**		
	A	**B**	**C**	**D**
Description	Monthly Take Home Amounts	Adjust Amount To:	Reason for Changing	Final Budget Amounts
1				
2				
3				
4				
5				
6				
Other Income:				
7				
8				
9				
10				
11 Total Spendable Income for Month (Add 1-10)				
Budgeted Expenses:		**Budget Adjustment**		
Description	Monthly Amount	Adjust Amount To:	Reason for Changing	Final Budget Amounts
12				
13				
14				
15				
16				
17				
18				
19				
20				
21				
22				
23				
24				
25				
26				
27				
28				
29				
30				
31				
32				
33				
34				
35				
36				
37				
38				
39				
40				
41				
42				
43				
44				
45				
46				
47 Total Expenses for Month (Add 12 - 46)				
48 Plus = Excess / (Minus) = Shortage (11 minus 47)				

143

Budgeting and Money Management - The Basics

Budgeting and Money Management - The Basics

Monthly Budget Worksheet - Budget Snapshot		**Month:**			
Budgeted Income:		**Budget Adjustment**			
	A	B	C		D
Description	Monthly Take Home Amounts	Adjust Amount To:	Reason for Changing		Final Budget Amounts
1					
2					
3					
4					
5					
6					
Other Income:					
7					
8					
9					
10					
11 Total Spendable Income for Month (Add 1-10)					
Budgeted Expenses:		**Budget Adjustment**			
Description	Monthly Amount	Adjust Amount To:	Reason for Changing		Final Budget Amounts
12					
13					
14					
15					
16					
17					
18					
19					
20					
21					
22					
23					
24					
25					
26					
27					
28					
29					
30					
31					
32					
33					
34					
35					
36					
37					
38					
39					
40					
41					
42					
43					
44					
45					
46					
47 Total Expenses for Month (Add 12 - 46)					
48 Plus = Excess / (Minus) = Shortage (11 minus 47)					

145

Budgeting and Money Management - The Basics

Budgeting and Money Management - The Basics

Monthly Budget Worksheet - Budget Snapshot	Month:			
Budgeted Income:		**Budget Adjustment**		
	A	B	C	D
Description	Monthly Take Home Amounts	Adjust Amount To:	Reason for Changing	Final Budget Amounts
1				
2				
3				
4				
5				
6				
Other Income:				
7				
8				
9				
10				
11 Total Spendable Income for Month (Add 1-10)				
Budgeted Expenses:		**Budget Adjustment**		
Description	Monthly Amount	Adjust Amount To:	Reason for Changing	Final Budget Amounts
12				
13				
14				
15				
16				
17				
18				
19				
20				
21				
22				
23				
24				
25				
26				
27				
28				
29				
30				
31				
32				
33				
34				
35				
36				
37				
38				
39				
40				
41				
42				
43				
44				
45				
46				
47 Total Expenses for Month (Add 12 - 46)				
48 Plus = Excess / (Minus) = Shortage (11 minus 47)				

www.ingramcontent.com/pod-product-compliance
Lightning Source LLC
Chambersburg PA
CBHW051918170526
45168CB00001B/440